HAMP

A MISCELLANY

Compiled by Julia Skinner

With particular reference to the work of John Bainbridge,
Nick Channer and Sarah Quail

THE FRANCIS FRITH COLLECTION

www.francisfrith.com

First published in the United Kingdom in 2011 by The Francis Frith Collection®

This edition published exclusively for Bradwell Books in 2013
For trade enquiries see: www.bradwellbooks.com or tel: 0800 834 920
ISBN 978-1-84589-566-2

British Library Cataloguing in Publication Data

Did You Know? Hampshire - A Miscellany
Compiled by Julia Skinner
With particular reference to the work of John Bainbridge, Nick Channer and Sarah Quail

The Francis Frith Collection
6 Oakley Business Park,
Wylye Road, Dinton,
Wiltshire SP3 5EU
Tel: +44 (0) 1722 716 376
Email: info@francisfrith.co.uk
www.francisfrith.com

Printed and bound in Malaysia
Contains material sourced from responsibly managed forests

Front Cover: **ANDOVER, ANTON MILL 1906** 54631p
Frontispiece: **CHILBOLTON, THE SEVEN STARS (NOW THE MAYFLY)
      TESTCOMBE c1907** C22730I

The colour-tinting is for illustrative purposes only, and is not intended to be historically accurate

CONTENTS

INTRODUCTION

The name of Hampshire derives from the Saxon name for Southampton of 'Hamtun', and was first recorded in AD755 as 'Hamtunscir'. The county later became known as Hamptonshire or even Southamptonshire, and the name of the administrative county was only changed from 'County of Southampton' to 'County of Hampshire' in 1959. However, despite the historic link with Southampton in the county's name, the county town of Hampshire is Winchester.

Few counties in the south of England offer such diversity of scenery as Hampshire. Much remains unspoilt, and embodies the heart and soul of the English countryside, with charming villages, rolling farmland, scenic forests and gentle river valleys. The country towns may have expanded over the years but their busy, colourful market squares survive. And, of course, there is the county's long coastline, rich with monuments to the past and reminders of how this country has defended itself over the centuries. To the west of the county lies the New Forest. Now a National Park, it is an important environment of woodland pasture, heaths, bogs, coppices and timber plantations. Other Hampshire forests are the Alice Holt Forest, adjacent to the Surrey border, and the Queen Elizabeth Country Park, north of Portsmouth, which are now popular amenity areas with many attractions for walkers and cyclists.

Hampshire includes three unique cities, Winchester, Southampton and Portsmouth. Winchester recalls the past at every turn and round every corner. There are many historic buildings within the city boundaries but the pride of Winchester is its magnificent cathedral. Southampton is a fascinating mix of ancient and modern; the city has much more to offer besides its sprawling docks and busy waterfront and is best explored on foot. Portsmouth, described in ancient times as 'the glory and the bulwark of these ancient kingdoms', is renowned for its association with the navy and its historic naval dockyard. Now, Portsmouth's most recent landmark of the Spinnaker Tower allows visitors to climb over 360ft and look out across the panorama of Hampshire's coast.

PORTSMOUTH, THE SPINNAKER TOWER 2005 P100714

HAMPSHIRE DIALECT WORDS AND PHRASES

'Ackled' - not working properly, as in 'It doesn't ackle'.

'Cackleberries' - eggs.

'Feeling lear' - feeling hungry.

'Foisty' - damp or musty.

'Gallibagger' - scarecrow.

'Lairy' or *'lair'* - cheeky, rude or aggressive.

'Not too dusty' - when something is okay, acceptable.

'Puggled' - confused or daft, as when someone does something silly.

'Scabs' - a local name in the Portsmouth area for winkles.

'Sherricking' - a good telling off.

'Shrammed' - cold, shivery, frozen through, as in 'feeling shrammed'.

'Skait' or *'skate'* - a sailor.

'Squinny' - complain. Used either as a verb, as in 'don't squinny' (don't complain) or an adjective, as in 'she's really squinny' (she complains a lot).

'Winty' - weather that is a bit windy and a bit wintery.

Superstitions lingered in the New Forest longer than in many places and are still recounted. Ill-fortune is still occasionally blamed upon a mischievous elf called Laurence. The old saying **'He's got a touch of Laurence'** implies lazy behaviour.

HAUNTED HAMPSHIRE

One of Portsmouth's most famous haunted buildings is Wymering Manor. It was investigated by television's 'Most Haunted Live' programme in 2006, when cold spots, strange tapping noises, and the sound of a baby crying were amongst the phenomena reported by the team. Amongst other locations in Portsmouth said to be haunted are the Theatre Royal, where the ghost of an actor who killed himself in his dressing room in the 1880s is said to roam the building, particularly at the back of the auditorium, and the building now known as Buckingham House in the High Street, which was the scene in 1628 of the assassination of the Duke of Buckingham by James Felton, a discontented naval officer. Felton was subsequently hanged and gibbeted on Southsea Common, and the building has been reputed to be haunted ever since, with reports of strange noises including terrifying groans, light orbs and sudden changes in temperature.

Southampton's Mayflower Theatre in Commercial Road has a mysterious ghost story: the figure of an old man who sits in a wicker chair has been seen backstage. Another ghost in the city is said to haunt the Dolphin Hotel in the High Street, reputedly the ghost of a cleaner called Molly who glides along the corridors with her legs below floor level.

The Eclipse Inn in The Square at Winchester is one of the city's most famous haunted sites, said to be roamed by the shade of Dame Alice Lisle of Moyles Court, near Ringwood, who spent her last few days in this inn before her execution in 1685. She was condemned to death by the notoriously savage Judge Jeffreys for allegedly harbouring two fugitives from the Monmouth rebellion, one of the first victims of his 'Bloody Assizes'. The scaffold for her execution was erected against the front of the inn, onto which the 71-year-old Lady Lisle stepped from an upstairs window. A plaque in The Square commemorates the event.

WINCHESTER, BUTTER CROSS 1899 43677

HAMPSHIRE MISCELLANY

At the time of the Roman invasion of Britain, the Winchester area
was a stronghold of the Iron Age tribe known as the Belgae. The
Romans named their market town beside the Itchen after them,
calling it 'Venta Belgarum', or 'the town of the Belgae'. Later, the
Hampshire area was settled by Jutes and Saxons. They called the
old Roman town at Winchester a 'caester', and changed its name to
'Venta Caester'. Over time this became 'Wintancaester', and eventually
'Winchester', the capital of the kingdom of Wessex, and then of
Anglo-Saxon England. It was the principal city of King Alfred the
Great, who ruled between AD871 and AD899 and spent long years
of his reign fending off the Danes. King Alfred is commemorated in
Winchester with a dramatic bronze statue by Hamo Thorneycroft,
erected in 1901, which occupies a prominent site in Broadway.

**WINCHESTER
KING ALFRED'S STATUE
1901** 43677A

WINCHESTER, THE GREAT HALL AND THE ROUND TABLE 1912
64458

After the Norman Conquest of 1066, William the Conqueror retained
Winchester as his capital and built a castle and a royal palace there.
His great survey of England known as the Domesday Book was
compiled in Winchester in 1086. In the 13th century Winchester's
castle was rebuilt by King Henry III. Oliver Cromwell's forces
destroyed the castle during the Civil War, leaving only the Great Hall,
considered by many to be the best medieval hall in the country after
Westminster Hall. A famous feature of the Great Hall is the Round
Table, traditionally associated with the legendary King Arthur and
his knights, which hangs on the west wall. Supposedly made by the
wizard Merlin, the Round Table has hung in Winchester's Great Hall
for some 600 years. In fact, it was made in the late 13th century and
restored in Tudor times, when the face of the young Henry VIII was
added to the portrait of King Arthur.

Winchester's huge cathedral was begun in 1079 and consecrated in 1093, but the building was consistently altered up till the 16th century. Inside the cathedral is a stunning 12th-century black marble font, carved with scenes from the life of St Nicholas. There are also magnificent 14th-century carved stalls and a beautiful 15th-century reredos, as well as other treasures such as the Winchester Bible in the Cathedral Library, which dates from the 12th century and is probably the finest illustrated book in England. In medieval times, pilgrims came to pray at the shrine of St Swithun in the cathedral. St Swithun is depicted on the altar screen with a pile of eggs at his feet, and the candlesticks on his shrine have a broken eggshell at each base. These are references to a miracle said to have been performed by the saint, when he mended a basket of eggs that had been dropped by a woman bringing them to market after she was bumped into by a short-sighted monk. St Swithun miraculously made the eggs whole again, to the delight of the farmer's wife.

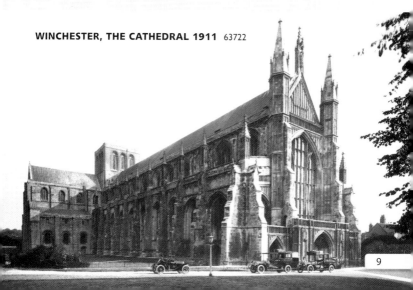

WINCHESTER, THE CATHEDRAL 1911 63722

The Hospital of St Cross near Winchester was founded by Bishop Henry de Blois in 1136, and is the oldest almshouse in England. It was originally founded to provide for the daily feeding of 100 poor men, and to house, clothe and feed 'thirteen poor impotent men, so reduced in strength as rarely or never to be able to raise themselves without the assistance of another'. By the rules of the foundation of St Cross Hospital, for eight centuries travellers have been given bread and ale on demand – a custom known as 'the Wayfarer's Dole'. Even today, if you visit St Cross Hospital and ask, you will be given a portion of bread and a beaker of ale by one of the pensioners.

Another ancient custom takes place at Tichborne, east of Winchester, which dates from the mid 12th century. The 'Tichborne Dole' originated in the deathbed request made by Lady Mabelle de Tichborne, to her husband that he should set aside the produce of some of his land for the relief of the poor. He agreed to grant as much land as she could crawl around during the time it took a firebrand to burn. Lady Mabelle managed to crawl around 20 acres before she died, and the land is still known as 'the Crawls' after her feat. The Tichborne Dole used to be loaves of bread but is now an allowance of flour, and is still distributed to villagers every year on March 25th.

A huge pyramidal monument on Farley Mount, west of Winchester, is a memorial to a horse, which is buried beneath it. A tablet inside records that Paulet St John was fox hunting in 1733 when his horse leapt into a chalk pit. Both horse and rider survived the 25ft fall, and went on to win the Hunter's Pale at the Worthy Down races the next year, the horse having been entered as 'Beware Chalk Pit'.

Bishop's Waltham gets its name from Henry of Blois, Bishop of Winchester, who built the bishop's palace there in the 12th century. Queen Mary I (Mary Tudor) stayed there before her marriage to Philip of Spain in Winchester Cathedral in 1554. The palace was destroyed in 1644, during the Civil War, and is now a ruin.

One of Hampshire's hidden treasures is the lovely Saxon church at Corhampton, north of Bishop's Waltham. The sundial on the south wall is divided not into 12 sections, as is usual today, but eight three-hour 'tides', representing the Saxon way of counting time (ie 'noontide'). The wall paintings probably date from the 12th century. Another interesting church in the area is that of St Peter and St Paul at Exton, which contains a delightful Jacobean altar, a 13th-century canopied piscina and a Victorian Early-English-style font. An unusual feature of its churchyard is a headstone depicting the Angel of Death summoning a book lover, who sits up in bed to face his final visitor.

The Church of St Mary and All Saints in Droxford has an unusual square stair-turret in the tower, thought to be unique in the country.

The church of St Nicholas at Wickham, south of Bishop's Waltham, is noted for its Uvedale monument of 1615, on which William Uvedale and his wife are depicted accompanied by their kneeling children. Wickham was the birthplace in 1324 of William of Wykeham, who founded Winchester College in 1382, one of the oldest public schools in England. Born the son of a serf, William of Wykeham rose to become Bishop of Winchester from 1367 to 1404 and also chancellor of England. Winchester College was originally founded to prepare 70 poor scholars for entry to New College, Oxford, which William of Wykeham also founded, and then for the priesthood. One of his sayings, 'Manners Maketh Man', is the motto of both Winchester College and New College, Oxford.

ANDOVER, HIGH STREET 1908 60092

Andover was an important centre for the textile trade in the past, as recalled by such place names in the town as Weavers Place, Rack Close and Silkweavers Road. Andover's parish church of St Mary was rebuilt in Neo-Gothic style in the 19th century, and has been described as the best Victorian church in Hampshire.

The church of St Mary at Abbotts Ann, south west of Andover, is famous for the medieval funeral custom still observed there of awarding a 'virgin's crown' at the funeral of any unmarried person of unblemished character who was born and baptised in the parish and who died there too. The crowns are made of hazel twigs, and decorated with paper rosettes and parchment gauntlets. They are suspended from the gallery of the church at the funeral and left there for about three weeks, so that all who enter the church must pass beneath. If no one disputes the deceased's good name in that time, the crown is taken down and hung on the wall on either side of the nave until it falls down through old age. At the time of writing (2011), the last crown was awarded in 1973.

Wherwell's now ruined priory was established as a house for nuns by the Saxon Queen Elfrida. According to a local folk tale, a toad once hatched a duck egg in the crypt of Wherwell Priory. The fierce creature that emerged, called a cockatrice, breathed the fire of a dragon and had the razor-sharp talons of a bird. It grew enormous and killed all who came near it, and the nuns cowered in terror. Eventually, one brave and ingenious villager approached the beast in its lair holding a shining polished shield in front of him. The beast was so enraged by its reflection in the shield that it launched an attack upon the imagined foe with such fury that it soon became exhausted. The man then entered the crypt and cut off the cockatrice's head. Andover museum has on display an old weather-vane fashioned in the form of the cockatrice, which once adorned the steeple of the church of St Peter and Holy Cross at Wherwell.

WHERWELL, THE VILLAGE 1901 46353

A feature of the Grosvenor Hotel in Stockbridge is its 'porte cochere' overhanging the pavement, which served two functions in stagecoaching days: those in the coach could alight and keep dry under its shelter, whilst travellers on top of the coach and the luggage could enter the building by a high level door. Nowadays, the upper storey of the porte cochere is used as the meeting room of the renowned Houghton Fishing Club, which is restricted to fewer than 20 members. The walls of its clubroom are covered with glass cases containing enormous stuffed brown trout, the fish for which the Test is famous.

STOCKBRIDGE, HIGH STREET c1955 S259062

The Wallop brook which joins the River Test south of Stockbridge runs through the three delightful villages of Over Wallop, Middle Wallop and Nether Wallop. Inside Nether Wallop's parish church of St Andrew are medieval wall paintings depicting St George fighting the dragon. Nether Wallop was used as the location for Miss Marple's home village of St Mary Mead in the BBC TV adaptations of Agatha Christie's crime novels in the 1980s and 90s that featured Joan Hickson as the eponymous amateur detective.

The River Test rises at Ashe, west of Basingstoke, and empties into Southampton Water, in the outskirts of Southampton. The railway line that used to follow the Test Valley from Andover through Fullerton, Stockbridge, and Romsey to Redbridge, on the outskirts of Southampton came to be known as the 'Sprat and Winkle' line, with seafood delivered by the line from Redbridge. Queen Victoria requested that royal trains used this route when she travelled to the Hampshire coast to go to Osborne House on the Isle of Wight. It had no smoky tunnels, and with superb views of the Test, she thought of the journey as just like 'going down the Nile'. The 'Sprat and Winkle' line was closed in 1964, and its 22-mile length became a walking route known as the Test Way, which can now be walked from Andover all the way to Southampton.

The great Norman church of Romsey Abbey is said to be the only Norman nunnery church still standing in England. The abbey was founded in AD907 by Edward the Elder, son of Alfred the Great, as a house for Benedictine nuns, but the main part of the building dates from the 12th century. The church is uniquely dedicated to St Mary and St Ethelflaeda. The nunnery was closed by Henry VIII in 1539, but the church was spared demolition as the people of Romsey were using it as their parish church and were able to raise the then huge sum of £100 demanded by the king for this most important building. The original Deed of Sale of the abbey to the town, with Henry VIII's signature, is on display in the small treasury in the south aisle of the church.

ROMSEY, THE PALMERSTON MONUMENT 1898 42103

Romsey prospered with the improved turnpike roads of the 18th and 19th centuries. The roads from Salisbury to Southampton and from Winchester to the west crossed the river here, and the coaching trade brought much business to the town's pubs and inns. There were around 40 or so public houses in Romsey at one time, and Romsey had a reputation for alcoholic over-indulgence in the past – until quite recent times there was a local saying for a drunken man that 'he must have been to Romsey'.

Romsey is famous for its associations with the third Lord Palmerston (1784-1865), Conservative Prime Minister during Queen Victoria's reign, and Admiral of the Fleet Earl Mountbatten of Burma (1900-1979) both of whom lived at the magnificent Palladian mansion of Broadlands (see opposite) just outside the town. An imposing bronze statue of Lord Palmerston by Matthew Noble surveys Romsey's Market Place.

Near Romsey is Embley Park. Now a school, it was the childhood home of Florence Nightingale, the creator of the modern nursing profession. As a young woman she spent three months at Salisbury Infirmary to train as a nurse and was horrified with the state of the hospital and the standard of nursing at that time. She became determined to raise the standards of medical care, and by the time the Crimean War was being fought in the 1850s, she had a decade of training behind her in various hospitals in Britain and on the Continent. Her work in the military hospitals during the war made her famous, and for the rest of her life she campaigned tirelessly to make nursing a respectable profession and improve hospital facilities, collecting statistics and making exhaustive reports which her friend Lord Palmerston of Broadlands passed on to the authorities. Florence Nightingale died in 1910 and was buried beside her parents in St Margaret's churchyard in East Wellow, near Romsey, escorted to her resting place by soldiers from the regiments that had served in the Crimea.

BROADLANDS 1898 42111

William the Conqueror created his 'New Forest' in Hampshire
as a hunting preserve in 1079. Near Cadnam is the Rufus Stone
which commemorates the death in the New Forest of William the
Conqueror's son and successor, William II (called William Rufus
because of his red hair) whilst out hunting in 1100, allegedly killed
by an arrow fired by Sir Walter Tyrrell which glanced either off a tree
or the back of a hunted stag before striking him down. Interestingly,
William Rufus's younger brother Richard had died in the New Forest
some years earlier, by strangulation after being caught up in the
boughs of a tree whilst hunting, as well as his nephew, also called
Richard (an illegitimate son of his elder brother Robert), who had
also been killed by a stray arrow in the forest – an uncanny trio of
coincidences...

The largest (and probably the oldest) oak tree in the New Forest is the
Knightwood Oak near Lyndhurst, which has a girth of 7.4 metres (over
24 feet). There is also a famous oak tree at Copythorne near Cadnam,
which defies nature by budding with leaves in midwinter, around
Christmas Day (grid reference SU 292 136).

The New Forest is now a National Park. Though there are woodlands a-
plenty, much of the region also comprises stretches of wild heathland
and the 'lawns', close-cropped by deer and the famous New Forest
ponies that roam freely throughout the region. All the ponies are
owned by someone, although they may stay out in the Forest all year
– the true New Forest pony can survive outdoors through all seasons,
eating holly and furze tops during the winter. The Verderers are the
officials who keep law and order in the forest, and their officers, called
Agisters, watch over the welfare of the animals that live there. The
Verderers' Court meets five times a year at Lyndhurst (the 'capital' of
the New Forest) to sort out Forest disputes.

The Royal Forests of the Norman and medieval period had their own set of harsh laws, as though they were separate kingdoms within the realm of England. Under Forest Law it was an offence for people living in the area to hunt, wound or kill the king's deer, and any dog over a certain size living within the forests had to be 'lawed' (or 'expediated'), which involved having three claws cut from within the pad of each forefoot, to lame the dog so that its owner could not use it for unlawful hunting. In the Verderers' Hall in Lyndhurst is a surviving 'dog stirrup' which was used to measure dogs; it measures 15cms (6 inches) in diameter, and only dogs small enough to pass through this device were allowed to roam the forest without mutilation.

LYNDHURST, HIGH STREET 1908 60106

An ancient common right claimed by people living in the New Forest is 'pannage', the right to turn out pigs into the forest to feed on beech mast and acorns for around 60 days from September to November – the so-called 'Pannage Month'. Acorns fall from oak trees at this time and green acorns are poisonous to deer and ponies, but are excellent for fattening pigs. At the end of the Pannage Month the acorns have turned brown and are safe for deer and other creatures to eat, and pigs are then excluded from the forest.

The strange creature depicted on 'The Trusty Servant' inn sign at Minstead in the New Forest is modelled on a picture in Winchester College. It is a composite of several animals symbolising the virtues embodied in the perfect servant: a pig for unfussiness in diet (with its snout locked for secrecy), an ass for patience, a stag for swiftness and a laden hand for hard work.

The name of Brockenhurst, in the south of the New Forest, means 'the badger's wood'. The churchyard of the parish church of St Nicholas in Brockenhurst includes a famous, intricately carved monument to Harry Mills, a renowned local character and snake-catcher, who died in 1905. He lived in a hut in the forest and made his living by catching adders, which he would kill and bake, and then make an ointment from their fat which he sold as a remedy for rheumatism, bruises and other ailments. The memorial shows him standing outside his forest hut, with a handful of snakes. He was a regular customer at the Railway Inn in the town, which is now called The Snakecatcher in his memory.

RINGWOOD, THE MILLSTREAM 1900 45027

Cut into the turf on Breamore Down north of Fordingbridge is a medieval 'miz-maze', a labyrinth of pathways thought to have been associated with an Augustine priory which once stood nearby. The monks probably used the miz-maze for religious purposes as a form of penance, crawling on their knees to the centre of the maze and then out again.

Ringwood lies beside the River Avon which is famous for a rare kind of eel, called locally a 'sniggle'; unlike the Common Eel, it has an elongated jaw and slender form. A local industry in Ringwood in the past was the manufacture of gloves known as 'Ringwoods', which were knitted by local women in their homes in a distinctive 'Ringwood' pattern: two rounds plain, one round rib. In the mid 20th century nearly 900 women were employed knitting the gloves for sale to London stores. Yellow cotton gloves were particularly popular with horse-riders. Commercial production ceased in the 1960s, when competition from cheap machine-made gloves from the Far East made the hand knitting of gloves uneconomical.

21

Southampton Water is the name given to the wide estuary of two of Hampshire's great rivers – the Test and the Itchen. At its lowest point Southampton Water is also joined by the River Hamble, before it meets the Solent off Hampshire's coast. The Solent is the strait of water between the Hampshire coast to the east and west of Southampton Water and the Isle of Wight. An unusual fact about the Solent is that the position of the Isle of Wight creates a sort of 'buffer', which causes the Solent to have four high tides a day.

Now an important yacht-building and sailing centre, Lymington was originally a Saxon port with a shipbuilding industry in operation between the Norman era and the 18th century, but between the 12th and 19th centuries the town's main industry was the manufacture of salt. Seawater was impounded in shallow tidal ponds, each about 20ft square, and left to evaporate until only a briny liquor remained. The brine was then pumped into iron or copper pans situated in barn-like buildings called boiling houses with coal-fired furnaces, where the water was boiled dry until only a deposit of salt crystals remained, which was scraped off and collected in baskets. Around 1800 Lymington was producing approximately 5,200 tons of salt a year and was the second largest producer in the kingdom after Liverpool, but shortly afterwards the industry declined following competition from Cheshire rock salt, and by 1825 only three salterns were operating.

The Chequers pub in Ridgeway Lane at Lower Woodside, on the edge of Lymington's salt marshes, gets its name from the saltmaking trade that was once so important to the area – the 'chequers' was the name for the local Salt Exchange Offices, or exchequer, which were at Lower Woodside Green in the days when salt was the key industry here.

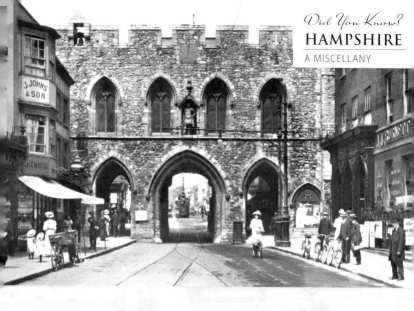

SOUTHAMPTON, BARGATE 1908 60428

In the early Middle Ages Southampton was known as just 'Hampton'. The name probably became Southampton to avoid the town being confused with Northampton. Cloth and wool were particularly important exports from medieval Southampton's busy port, and the town grew very wealthy. In 1338, French, Genoese and Sicilian raiders attacked Southampton, looting and burning the town. Amongst them was a pirate called Grimaldi, who used the plunder he took from the town to help found the principality of Monaco. Grimaldi is still the name of the Monaco royal family, and it could be said that the wealth of the principality was partly founded on Southampton silver. After this raid the town walls were rebuilt, and Southampton developed into one of the strongest fortresses in the land. The defensive town wall incorporated twenty-nine towers and seven gates. Extensive stretches of the medieval town walls survive today, and many of the towers and five of the seven gates are still standing.

Bargate in Southampton is one of the finest medieval gateways in the country, dating back to the late 12th century. It was originally built to guard the main road into Southampton. Characterised by pointed arches and fine stonework, the old gate also features a statue of George III, dressed in Classical style as a Roman. The photograph on page 23 shows Bargate as it looked in 1908. Notice the tram approaching in the background of this photograph – until the 1930s, specially designed trams with dome-shaped tops to fit the arch travelled through Bargate. The adjoining walls and buildings were subsequently destroyed so that traffic bypassed the gate.

Holy Rood Church at the bottom of Southampton's High Street was erected in 1320 and was known for centuries as 'the church of the sailors'. The church was badly damaged by enemy bombing in 1940 during the Second World War, but its ruins have been preserved by the people of the city as a memorial and garden of rest, dedicated to those who served in the Merchant Navy and lost their lives at sea.

Southampton was the home port of the ill-fated 'Titanic'. A small quayside memorial marks the spot where she was berthed prior to leaving on her doomed maiden voyage in April 1912. There are several poignant monuments around the city commemorating the crew and staff who served on the 'Titanic', many of whom were from Southampton – it has been estimated that around 500 local households lost a family member when the ship sank. As well as the memorial to the stewards, sailors and firemen who perished that can be found in the memorial garden of the ruined church of Holy Rood (see above), the 'Titanic' memorial in East Park recalls the engineer-officers who 'showed their high conception of duty and heroism by remaining at their posts'. There is also a memorial to the musicians who went down with the ship, which can be found at the junction of London Road and Cumberland Place, and a touching memorial in St Joseph's Church in Bugle Street commemorates the restaurant staff who died.

Southampton was granted city status in 1964, making it Hampshire's youngest city, but it has no cathedral. Its main church is St Mary's, in St Mary Street. Every four hours the clock on the tower of Southampton's Civic Centre plays the hymn 'O God Our Help In Ages Past', which was the work of the famous hymn-writer Isaac Watts, who was a native of Southampton. Watts is also commemorated in the city with a monument in Watts Park, which is named after him.

Alfred Hawthorne Hill, better known by his stage name of Benny Hill, was born in Southampton, in 1924 and started his career as an entertainer in an Eastleigh concert party. Before the Second World War he worked as a milkman in the Swaythling and Eastleigh area for Hanns Dairy, and in later life he immortalised Eastleigh when he wrote a song about his time as a milkman there which reached No 1 in 1971: 'And he galloped into Market Street with his badge upon his chest... His name was Ernie, and he drove the fastest milkcart in the west'. The connection is commemorated with a plaque on the Swan Centre in Eastleigh, which now stands on the site of Hanns Dairy.

SOUTHAMPTON, THE CIVIC CENTRE c1955 S151046

**FAREHAM, HENRY CORT
SCULPTURE PARK
'STILL MOVES'
2005** F103703

The old Market Hall which used to stand in the centre of Titchfield was probably built around 1612. This fine building with a timber framework and herring-bone brickwork was dismantled in 1971 and re-erected at the Weald and Downland Open Air Museum near Chichester in Sussex, where it can now be seen.

Part of the Market Quay shopping development in Fareham has been named Cremer Mall in remembrance of Sir William Randal Cremer, who in 1903 became the first British person to win the Nobel Prize for Peace. Cremer was born in a house in West Street in Fareham in 1828 and lived there until the 1840s. He overcome poverty and hardship in early life to became a great trade unionist, an influential Member of Parliament and an international peace activist who founded the Interparliamentary Union, which still operates today to enable nations to settle disputes by arbitration rather than violence.

Another famous name in Fareham's history is Henry Cort, who invented two processes that improved the efficiency of iron manufacture whilst he was working at Fontley Iron Mill in the 1780s. His puddling and grooved rolls processes helped establish the global supremacy of the British iron industry in the early 19th century, and earned him the sobriquet of 'The Father of the Iron Trade'. He is commemorated in Fareham in the names of Henry Cort Community College and Cort Way and with the Henry Cort Sculpture Park in the town centre, which consists of a number of distinctive modern sculptures using wrought iron. The rock and chain sculpture known as 'Still Moves' (F103703, opposite) symbolises the processes associated with Henry Cort. Iron ore is extracted from the rock and smelted in a blast furnace to form pig iron, which is then refined to form malleable or wrought iron in a puddling furnace. The iron is then rolled into bars and forged into chains (Cort made chains to supply to the navy). The sculpture shows iron appearing from the rock in a tangled mess before being made into chains that rise to the sky. The inscription in the rock reads: 'Nothing is created, everything is transformed.'

Gosport is sited on a peninsular on the western side of Portsmouth harbour, opposite Portsmouth. According to the town's motto, the name of Gosport comes from the words 'God's Port', which King Stephen supposedly used when he gave thanks in 1144 for making safe landing there in a storm. Sadly, this appears to have been a 19th-century invention. A disparaging nickname for Gosport, particularly used in Portsmouth, is 'Turktown', because there is a Turkish graveyard in the grounds of the Clayhall Royal Naval Cemetery at Haslar, with the graves of 26 Turkish sailors from two visiting ships who died of natural causes between 1850 and 1852.

Portchester Castle, on the north side of Portsmouth Harbour, was originally built in the late third century to help protect Roman Britain from North Sea pirates. The great walled fortress was part of a defensive line of similar forts – the forts of the 'Saxon Shore' – stretching along the coast from the Wash to the Solent. In the 11th and 12th centuries the walls were rebuilt and the Norman castle that we see on the site today was constructed.

Portsdown Hill rises above Portsmouth behind Portchester. In the second half of the 19th century, the Prime Minister Lord Palmerston was responsible for building a ring of forts around Portsmouth to protect the dockyard and the anchorage at Spithead against a perceived threat from France. A string of six polygonal forts along the top of Portsdown Hill were constructed, as well as four sea forts built on shoals to defend the Spithead anchorage, Portsmouth harbour and its entrance. There was much opposition to the project and its expense in Parliament, and the Chancellor, Mr Gladstone, threatened to resign over it, but Lord Palmerston declared that it would be better to lose Gladstone than lose Portsmouth. The project took over 20 years to complete, by which time the threat from France had disappeared, and the forts became known as 'Palmerston's Follies'.

A key seafaring city and naval port since early times, Portsmouth evolved over the years into southern England's largest and most important naval base. The first ship repair facilities were probably built here in the late 12th or early 13th century, and in the 16th century the Tudor kings, Henry VII and Henry VIII, constructed the first dry dock in the world here. By the end of the 17th century, Portsmouth was the most strongly defended town in the country, and the leading naval dockyard. Later the city played a key role in the defence of the British Empire, and became synonymous with the navy. Portsmouth's nickname is 'Pompey'. It is not the prerogative of the football club to call itself by this name – the town, too, is known the world over as Pompey, but no one is exactly sure why. The most plausible reason relates to the story of the Portsmouth-based sailors who scaled Pompey's pillar in Alexandria in Egypt in 1781 and toasted their success from the top with punch. Their efforts earned them the nickname 'the Pompey Boys'.

PORTSMOUTH, THE HARBOUR AND THE 'VICTORY' 1898 42705

PORTSMOUTH, GUILDHALL SQUARE 1892 30002

The original township of Portsmouth was established in the late 12th
century by a wealthy merchant and landowner called Jean de Gisors,
who was probably drawn to the site at the harbour mouth by its
potential for developing cross-channel trading links. A marketplace
was designated and settlers were encouraged to move into the town
in the hope of developing trade. There is a delightful depiction of
Jean de Gisors in a stained glass window in Portsmouth Cathedral
(formerly St Thomas's Church), which is the oldest surviving building
in Portsmouth; the original chancel and transepts are part of the
chapel built on his instructions in the 1180s. Portsmouth's founding
father also features in Dan Brown's blockbuster novel 'The Da
Vinci Code', as a member of the Order of Sion. However, there is no
foundation in this particular part of the story.

The Royal Garrison Church on Governor's Green in Portsmouth was a originally a medieval hospice known as the Domus Dei, or God's House, which provided accommodation for pilgrims and strangers, and cared for local people who needed nursing. The complex was dissolved in 1538 by Henry VIII, and in the late 16th century it became the residence of Portsmouth's Governor, and was known as the Governor's House. In due course, the site was cleared of all the ancillary buildings, leaving only the early 13th-century chapel, now the Royal Garrison Church. The church was partially destroyed by wartime bombing but has been left standing, its nave open to the skies, as a permanent war memorial.

The marriage of King Charles II and the Portuguese princess Catherine of Braganza took place in Portsmouth at the Domus Dei, then the Governor's residence, in 1662. The marriage could not take place in Portsmouth's parish church of St Thomas because that building had been badly damaged by Parliamentarian guns during the Civil War. The people of Portsmouth gave the newly-married couple a wedding gift of a silver and crystal salt-cellar, which the diarist Samuel Pepys described as 'a salt-sellar of silver, the walls of cristall, with four Eagles and four greyhounds standing up at top to bear up a dish – which endeed is one of the neatest pieces of plate that ever I saw'.

The 19th-century writer Charles Dickens was born at what is now 393 Old Commercial Road in Portsmouth in 1812. His father, John Dickens, was a clerk in the Navy Pay Office. The house where Charles Dickens was born is now The Charles Dickens Birthplace Museum, decorated and furnished in Regency style and with a small gallery of Dickens memorabilia.

SOUTHSEA, THE BEACH AND THE CLARENCE PIER 1890 22761

A vast throng of local people gathered on Southsea beach to bid farewell to their naval hero Lord Nelson when he left England for the last time on September 14th 1805. A few weeks later he died on board his flagship, HMS 'Victory', during the battle of Trafalgar, shot by an enemy sniper. For many years the 'Victory' was moored in Portsmouth harbour (as seen in the background of photograph 42705 on page 29) but in 1922 she was towed to her last berth in the dockyard, where she is still the flagship of the Commander-in-Chief, Naval Home Command, the oldest naval ship in the world still in commission, and Portsmouth's most popular visitor attraction. A visit to the ship gives a fascinating glimpse of what life was like for the 828 crew on board the ship in Nelson's time. The crew of the 'Victory' at the battle of Trafalgar was very cosmopolitan – there were men on board from America, Holland, Italy, Malta, Ireland, West Indies and France, as well as Britain.

Southsea can be said to be the birthplace of Sherlock Holmes. Arthur Conan Doyle lived and worked as a GP in Southsea between 1882 and 1890, and wrote the first book in his series about the fictional detective, 'A Study in Scarlet', whilst living there.

Several notable monuments can be seen on Clarence Esplanade at Southsea, including the striking Naval Memorial to ranks and ratings of Portsmouth who 'have no other grave than the sea'. There is also the D-Day memorial. During the Second World War, General Eisenhower's headquarters were at Southwick House, north of Portsmouth, and it was here that he gave his historic 'order to go', which launched the great invasion offensive to recapture Western Europe from Hitler's Germany – D-Day, code-named 'Operation Overlord'. Southwick House is used as the navigation school of the naval establishment that now surrounds it, but can be visited by prior appointment. Inside the house, the operation room with the board used to plot the progress of the D-Day operation is still intact. The D-Day forces deployed from bases all along the south coast of England, Portsmouth being the most important, and the story of the operation is told at Portsmouth's excellent D-Day Museum on Clarence Esplanade in Southsea. The centrepiece of the museum is the spectacular Overlord Embroidery, the 20th-century equivalent of the Bayeux Tapestry. It is 83 metres (272 feet) in length, and took five years to complete.

Havant is a busy little town overlooking Langstone Harbour, an unspoilt area of salt marsh islands, tidal creeks, sandbanks and mudflats, between Portsea Island and Hayling Island. Havant was once famous for its parchment making. It is claimed that the Magna Carta was written on Havant parchment, and the parchment used for the 1919 Treaty of Versailles after the First World War came from there.

PETERSFIELD, BUTSER ANCIENT FARM 2005 P48721

North of Waterlooville, the Bat and Ball Inn at Broadhalfpenny
Down near Hambledon stands opposite one of the oldest cricket
pitches in the country, where a granite monument inscribed with
two cricket bats, a ball and a set of wickets marks the site of the
ground of the Hambledon Cricket Club circa 1750-1787. The cricket
club's secretary was Richard Nyren, landlord of the Bat and Ball, who
formulated many of the rules of the game still in force today. It was at
Hambledon, too, that in 1807 Christina Willes, 'to avoid entanglement
with her voluminous skirt, bowled around-arm to a batsman of
Hambledon, and thus started such bowling in due course for all who
played the game'.

A few miles south of Petersfield, off the A3, is the Butser Ancient Farm,
a replica of an Iron Age farm from around 300BC with crops and
livestock from that time. The Ancient Farm is open to the public and
special open days are held regularly when 'living history' teams of
actors show what it was like to be an inhabitant of Iron Age Britain.

Petersfield's best-known landmark is the statue of King William III in the Market Square; it is in Classical style, based on the statue of Marcus Aurelius in Rome, and portrays the king dressed as a Roman emperor. One of Petersfield's famous citizens in the past was John Goodyer, who in the 17th century was one of England's foremost botanists; his name is commemorated in the 40 species of 'goodyera', otherwise known as the jewel orchid. He lived in a house on The Spain now known as Goodyers, which bears a plaque commemorating him. In 1907 a protection order was discovered under the floorboards of the house, given to John Goodyer by the Royalist general Lord Hopton during the Civil War of the 17th century. At that time of the Civil War crops were failing, and both Royalists and Parliamentarians needed John Goodyer's botanical expertise. The placename of The Spain in Petersfield probably means that the better-off people who lived there in the past could afford to have the roofs of their houses tiled, rather than thatched, since 'Spayne' is an old name for a tile.

PETERSFIELD, MARKET PLACE c1950 P48009

The poet Edward Thomas (1878-1917) came to live in east Hampshire in 1906, making his home in a cottage at Steep, north-east of Petersfield. He loved the area dearly and was moved to write about it in his work, inspired by the beauty of the beech hangers of the area and the distant downland glimpses. The Shoulder of Mutton Hill near Steep is the setting for the Poet Stone, a sarsen stone dedicated to the memory of Edward Thomas, who was killed in the First World War. He is also commemorated with a memorial window in All Saints' Church at Steep, which was designed and engraved by Laurence Whistler.

LIPHOOK, THE TOWN 1911 63110

The first dedicated post office in England opened in 1845 in Hampshire, at Kings Worthy near Winchester. In the 1890s Flora Timms came to Grayshott in Hampshire to work at the post office there, and also worked at the post office in Yateley. She is better known now by her married name of Flora Thompson, author of the 'Lark Rise to Candleford' trilogy of books in which she gives a (fictionalised) picture of working in a rural post office in the late 19th and early 20th centuries. She came back to Hampshire in 1916 when her husband, John Thompson, was appointed the local postmaster at Liphook, and lived in the town until 1928.

The pioneering naturalist and ornithologist Gilbert White was born in Selborne, near Alton, in 1720 and lived in the village for most of his life. His world-famous book, 'The Natural History and Antiquities of Selborne', is a compilaton of his letters to Thomas Pennant, a leading zoologist of the day, and Daines Barrington, a Fellow of the Royal Society, in which he recorded his discoveries about local birds, animals and plants. Gilbert White had a great respect for nature and believed in distinguishing birds by observation rather than by collecting specimens. He is regarded by many people as England's first ecologist. His former home at Selborne, The Wakes, now houses the Gilbert White Museum, and there is a memorial window to him in St Mary's church in the village, showing St Francis of Assisi feeding the birds – 64 birds are depicted in it.

Another literary name with Hampshire connections is Jane Austen. Chawton, near Alton, is where she made her last home and where she wrote 'Mansfield Park', 'Emma' and 'Persuasion'. The house where she lived for the last eight years of her life, from 1809 until 1817, is now a museum and contains Jane's writing table, as well as a collection of documents and letters.

ALTON, HIGH STREET 1898 42266

The cloth industry was of great importance to Alton in the medieval and early post-medieval periods, and a source of the town's early wealth. Much of the cloth, mainly kersey (a coarse-ribbed woollen cloth), came from surrounding settlements, such as Headley, Petersfield and East Meon, but in Alton itself a dye-house stood beside the River Wey. Another important local industry in the Alton area in the past was brewing, which developed a major agricultural activity in the villages around the town, in the form of hop growing. The hop, used for flavouring and preserving beer, was a major crop in this part of the world in the 18th, 19th and 20th centuries, and the last commercial hop-gardens in the area only closed in quite recent years. Evidence of the industry can be seen in many places in the form of the former hop-kilns, now often converted into housing. Hops grown in the villages around Alton were said to be second only to Farnham hops in quality and in the prices commanded.

Before assuming the role of the first military town in Britain, Aldershot was no more than a small village, close to an area of open heathland. Then in 1854 the Army decided to establish a permanent camp in the area. The first, tented, military encampment of 1854 soon gave way to rows of wooden huts arranged in 'Lines', designated A to Z, each one providing accommodation for a battalion, or equivalent. As seen in the photograph below, the commanding officer's accommodation was equally modest. The wooden huts of the 'Lines' gave way in the 1890s to brick-built huts which, in turn, have now largely been demolished and replaced by modern buildings. One of Aldershot's most famous landmarks is Matthew Wyatt's magnificent bronze statue of the Duke of Wellington, victor of the battle of Waterloo in 1815, seated on his horse, Copenhagen. The statue originally stood at Hyde Park Corner in London. In 1885 it was dismantled and transported to Aldershot, where it was re-erected on Round Hill.

ALDERSHOT
OFFICER COMMANDING'S RESIDENCE
1892 31117

Despite the speedy development of Farnborough in the 19th and 20th centuries, the town has historic origins. The oldest building in Farnborough, the parish church of St Peter, dates from about 1200, although a Saxon church may have occupied the site before then. Inside the church there are wall paintings of three female saints dating from when the church was first built.

The removal of the Army Balloon Factory from Aldershot to Farnborough in 1905 was certainly Farnborough's gain. The Army Balloon Factory evolved into the Royal Aircraft Factory in 1911, before becoming the Royal Aircraft Establishment in 1918. Many notable events took place there over the years, including when 'Colonel' Samuel Franklin Cody made the first powered flight in Great Britain in 1908. Ten years later, on 1st April 1918, the Royal Air Force was born in Farnborough, the product of the union between the Royal Flying Corps and the Royal Naval Air Service.

FARNBOROUGH, LYNCHFORD ROAD 1924 75506A

FLEET, MARKET SQUARE 1908 60064

Between Fleet and Cove lies Fleet Pond, the largest freshwater pond in the county – it is three quarters of a mile long, and covers about 130 acres. The building of the railway station at Fleet in 1847 meant that the attractions of Fleet Pond were now readily available to day-trippers coming down from London; indeed, the station was known as Fleet Pond Station until 1869. The development of Fleet really began in earnest from 1878 when Mr Henry Brake of Farnborough bought nearly 250 acres of heathland in the area. Roads were laid out in American grid fashion, and plots of land were sold off on easy terms, which quickly led to an increase in the local population. Considered to be Fleet's most famous landmark, the dome on the building on the left of the above photograph is part of the old Oakleys department store. The store opened in 1885 and sold everything from groceries to bicycles, millinery and furniture. There was also an off-licence and funeral furnishing department. Oakleys closed in the late 1950s.

FLEET, BOATING ON THE BASINGSTOKE CANAL 1908 60081x

The Basingstoke Canal opened in 1794. This 37 miles of waterway from its junction with the River Wey navigation at West Byfleet linked Basingstoke with London. It was built with the intention of boosting local trade by providing cheap transport for agricultural goods and locally produced timber, bricks and chalk, but the canal's construction costs were twice the estimate, and it was never commercially viable. The last commercial craft on the canal operated in 1950, and the canal then became derelict. The Surrey and Hampshire Canal Society was formed in 1966 to campaign for the canal's restoration and public ownership. This goal was achieved when Surrey and Hampshire County Councils purchased it in 1974, and restoration work began in earnest. It was officially reopened in 1991, and the canal is again navigable from Greywell Tunnel near Odiham to the River Wey.

Odiham's long, wide High Street has the finest range of historic buildings of any town in Hampshire. Dating from 1300, they are nearly all listed buildings. Prior to Georgian and Victorian 'modernisation', at least 20 of the timber-framed buildings were jettied (ie, with an overhanging upper storey). A glance at the side walls of some of the buildings gives an indication of their earlier origins. The size and quality of the buildings are indications of the wealth and prosperity of Odiham in the medieval period. During the Napoleonic Wars a number of French prisoners of war were on parole in Odiham, living in cottages in the old chalk pit near the town, and the parish churchyard contains the graves of several French prisoners who died during their time there.

The now-ruined Odiham Castle at North Warnborough is the only castle in England with an octagonal keep. King John was a regular visitor, and left from Odiham Castle in 1215 to affix his seal to the Magna Carta at Runnymede in Surrey.

ODIHAM, THE GEORGE HOTEL 1924 75277

Despite its rapid development in the 20th century, Basingstoke still has some interesting and distinctive old buildings, particularly in Winchester Street and London Street. Basingstoke also has perhaps the finest of Hampshire's Perpendicular churches, the Church of St Michael the Archangel – its tower can be seen peeping above the town's rooftops in the photograph below.

In the 19th century a draper in Basingstoke devised a method of waterproofing yarn and cloth, after noticing that a local shepherd's smock became waterproof as a result of absorbing oil from the wool of his sheep. He set up a factory in the town to manufacture his cloth, marketed it successfully and made his fortune. His name was Thomas Burberry, and he called his waterproofed cloth 'Gabardine'.

BASINGSTOKE, CHURCH STREET 1904 52129

44

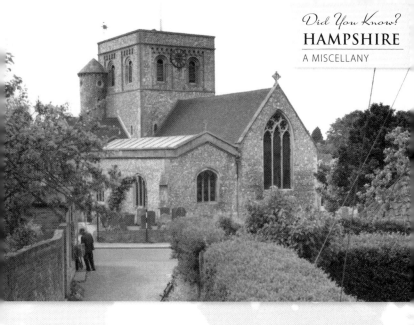

KINGSCLERE, ST MARY'S CHURCH c1960 KI40081

The village church of St Mary in the north Hampshire village of Kingsclere, north west of Basingstoke, contains magnificent monuments to Sir Henry Kingsmill and his wife Lady Bridget, but the church is also famous for a most unusual decoration, a weather-vane in the shape of a bed-bug, seen above on the left hand side of the tower in this view. It is a very tasteful bed-bug, with six little crosses for legs, and another for its tail, but a bed-bug it definitely is. The story goes that back in the early 13th century King John was hunting in the area. A thick fog prevented him returning to his hunting lodge on Cottington Hill and he had to spend the night at the local inn in Kingsclere, where his rest was much disturbed by the depredations of bed-bugs on the royal person. King John was so annoyed by his disturbed night that he commanded an effigy of a bed-bug be erected on the church tower, and a depiction of the insect remains there to this day.

SPORTING HAMPSHIRE

Hayling Island, located between Langstone Harbour and Chichester Harbour, was where board sailing was invented. This was confirmed by a High Court ruling in 1982 stating that Peter Chilvers invented the sail board at Hayling in 1958 when, as a boy of ten, he used a sheet of plywood, a tent fly sheet, a pole and some curtain rings to sail up an island creek.

Southampton Football Club moved to its new ground at St Mary's in 2001 from its former home at The Dell. The name of Southampton's St Mary's stadium is in part a reference back to the original St Mary's football club, from which Southampton Football Club developed. To date (2011), Southampton Football Club has played in four FA Cup finals, losing three and winning once. Each of these appearances has been of historic interest. In the first two final matches (1900 and 1902) the club were not even members of the Football League, being in the Southern League. Unfortunately they were not able to match Tottenham's record of being the only non-league team to win the trophy. The 1976 win, over Manchester United, was famous for being one of the greatest upsets in the history of the FA Cup. The only (winning) goal was, ironically, scored by a Portsmouth-born player, Bobby Stokes. It was his, and the club's, finest hour – sadly, he died tragically young in 1995. The 2003 defeat, also a 1-0 scoreline, against Arsenal was notable for being the first FA Cup final played under a closed roof, the game being held at the Millennium Stadium in Cardiff.

The Olympic athlete Roger Black was born in Portsmouth in 1966, and attended Portsmouth Grammar School where he was head boy. Amongst his impressive medal collection are a silver medal for the 400m from the 1996 Olympics in Atlanta, USA and another silver medal from the 1997 World Championships for the 4 x 400m relay.

The rivalry between Southampton and Portsmouth Football Clubs is well-known, but in former years there was equal rivalry between Portsmouth and Plymouth Argyle, referred to variously as the Naval Derby, the Dockyard Derby or the Battle of the Ports.

The colour of Portsmouth Football Club's original kit was salmon pink! It changed to the familiar royal blue shirts and white shorts in 1911. One of the favourite chants sung by Portsmouth FC supporters around Fratton Park is the Pompey Chimes ('Play up Pompey, Pompey play up'). This originated with the Royal Artillery, a football team who played many of their home games at the United Services ground in Burnaby Road in the 1890s. Referees at these matches used the sound of the striking of the Guildhall clock to mark the end of the match at 4pm. The crowd would chant in time with the clock as it chimed the hour to encourage the referee to blow the final whistle. After the Royal Artillery were expelled from the FA Amateur Cup in the 1898-99 season many of their supporters turned to Portsmouth FC instead, bringing their Chimes chant with them.

Portsmouth-born Katy Sexton MBE, a member of Portsmouth Northsea Swimming Club, became the first British female swimmer to win an individual gold medal at the 2003 World Championships in Barcelona in the 200m backstroke event.

The River Hamble empties into Southampton Water at Hamble-le-Rice, which has long been famous as a yachting centre. Once a year, members of the Royal Southern Yacht Club at Hamble and the Island Sailing Club on the Isle of Wight take part in one of Britain's strangest events – a cricket match played in the middle of the Solent! For about one hour each year the Brambles sandbank appears in the Solent, about halfway between Southampton and the Isle of Wight. The two teams head out to the sandbank, many dressed appropriately in cricket whites, and play a quick game of cricket before the sea reclaims the pitch. Both teams then adjourn to the Isle of Wight for a celebratory dinner.

QUIZ QUESTIONS

Answers on page 52.

1. What is the nickname for a person born and living in Hampshire?

2. Which comic opera by Gilbert & Sullivan is set in Portsmouth Harbour?

3. What were Fareham Reds?

4. Why is Southampton's main theatre called The Mayflower Theatre?

5. Whereabouts in Hampshire can you find a pub named after a strawberry?

6. In medieval times, pilgrims came from all over Europe to pay homage at the shrine of St Swithun in Winchester Cathedral. He was a former Bishop of Winchester who was known for his lack of pomp and ostentation. After he died in AD862 he was buried in the churchyard as he had requested, saying that he wanted the rain to fall on him, but over a century later, his remains were moved from their original resting-place to his shrine inside the cathedral. After this was done, there was a period of rain that lasted 40 days; it was believed that the saint was displeased with his bones being moved and had protested by 'weeping'. There is an old saying that if it rains on St Swithun's Day, it will continue to rain for the next 40 days – but when is St Swithun's Day?

7. What is the connection between Hampshire, the popular TV drama series 'Downton Abbey', and the Egyptian Boy Pharaoh Tutankhamun?

8. What is the name of the main ground of Hampshire County Cricket Club?

9. Who were Edward, Humphrey, Alice and Edith Beverley?

10. To date (2011) Portsmouth Football Club has won the FA Cup twice in its history. In 1939 The Blues beat Wolves 4-1 to win the trophy, and in the 2007/8 season they beat Cardiff City 1-0. However, Portsmouth can claim to have held the FA Cup for a longer period than any football club – why is that?

EVERSLEY, THE WHITE HART 1906 57011

RECIPE

WATERCRESS SOUP

Hampshire is one of the UK's main areas for the production of watercress, which is widely grown in the area around Winchester. The restored and privately owned steam railway running between Alresford and Alton is known as 'The Watercress Line', as it was once a vital link for the watercress industry. At one time, the line would carry upwards of 30 ton of watercress a week to the London market from Alresford alone. Watercress can be eaten raw as a salad or in sandwiches and it is traditionally used in Hampshire to make a creamy sauce to accompany freshwater fish, especially the trout that the county's rivers are renowned for. However, it is most famous for making a delicious soup.

> 50g/2oz butter
> 2 bunches of watercress with their stalks removed,
>   washed and chopped (but reserve a few sprigs
>   to garnish the soup)
> 1 medium onion, chopped
> 25g/1oz plain flour
> 600ml/1 pint milk
> 450ml/ ¾ pint chicken or vegetable stock
> 6 tablespoonfuls single cream

Melt the butter in a large pan, and gently fry the watercress and onion for a few minutes until softened. Stir in the flour and cook for a further one minute. Slowly stir in the milk, a little at a time, and then the stock. Bring to the boil, stirring all the time, until thickened, then cover and simmer gently for 30 minutes. Remove from the heat and cool for a few minutes, then liquidize. Before serving, add the cream and reheat gently, taking care not to allow the soup to boil. Serve with a swirl of cream and a sprig of watercress leaves to garnish.

RECIPE

HAMPSHIRE BACON PUDDING

This filling suet pudding was traditionally served with mashed potatoes, mashed swede and greens, like cabbage or kale.

> 225g/8oz plain flour
> Half a teaspoonful of baking powder
> Half a teaspoonful of salt
> 115g/4oz shredded suet
> 2 onions, finely sliced
> 6 bacon rashers, rinded but left whole
> Half a teaspoonful of dried sage, finely chopped
> Freshly ground black pepper to taste

Sift the flour, baking powder and salt into a bowl. Mix in the suet, then bind with a little water, to form a firm dough. Knead the dough until it is smooth, then roll it out into an oblong shape. Cover the dough with the bacon rashers, then cover the bacon with the sliced onions, leaving a margin around the edge. Sprinkle with the sage, then season to taste with pepper (you should not need to add salt, as the bacon will already be salty). Dampen the edges and roll it all up like a Swiss roll. Wet the ends, and pinch them together firmly to seal them. Loosely wrap the roll in a piece of buttered, pleated greaseproof paper and then in a further piece of buttered, pleated foil (this allows room for expansion during cooking), seal the ends of the wrapping well and tie with string. Fill the bottom half of a steamer or large saucepan with water and bring it to the boil. Put in the pudding, cover the pan with the lid and steam the pudding over boiling water for 2½ - 3 hours, topping up the pan with more boiling water if necessary, to ensure it does not boil dry. When cooked, lift out the pudding, unwrap, and place on an ovenproof serving dish in a pre-heated oven for 5 minutes to finish, at 180°C/350°F/Gas Mark 4. Serve cut into slices.

QUIZ ANSWERS

1. The nickname for a Hampshire-born local person is a 'Hampshire Hog'.

2. HMS 'Pinafore'.

3. Fareham was once famous for its bricks made of local clay, which were known as 'Fareham Reds'. They were renowned for their durability and quality, and were sent all over the country. The Royal Albert Hall in London was built using 'Fareham Reds'.

4. The name of Southampton's Mayflower Theatre commemorates the fact that the 'Mayflower' and the 'Speedwell' departed from Southampton in August 1620 with the group of puritan emigrants to the New World in America known as the Pilgrim Fathers. The 'Mayflower' is also commemorated in Southampton with the Pilgrim Fathers' Monument on Town Quay, which is crowned by a copper model of the 'Mayflower' in the form of a weathervane.

5. At Locks Heath, west of Fareham, where the Sir Joseph Paxton pub in Hunts Pond Road is not only named after the famous 19th-century botanist, but also commemorates the variety of strawberry he developed. From the 1860s until the mid 20th century, there was an important local strawberry-growing industry in the Locks Heath area. The Sir Joseph Paxton strawberry was particularly popular, and was so widely grown in Locks Heath that the nickname of 'Joe pickers' was given to the itinerant strawberry pickers employed to harvest the fruit during the strawberry season.

6. St Swithun's Day is 15th July.

7. The 'real' Downton Abbey is Highclere Castle in the extreme north of Hampshire, near Newbury, which was used as the location for the stately home of the popular TV drama series. Highclere Castle is the country seat of the Earls of Carnarvon. It was the 5th Earl of Carnarvon who, along with his archaeological colleague Howard Carter, discovered the tomb of the Egyptian Boy Pharaoh Tutankhamun in 1922.

8. The main ground of Hampshire County Cricket Club is the Rose Bowl at West End near Southampton. The Rose Bowl was newly built in 2001 and is a state of the art stadium, one of only two modern purpose-built cricket grounds in the country.

9. They were 'The Children of the New Forest', the classic children's adventure story set in the New Forest during the time of the Civil War and the Commonwealth. It was written by Captain Frederick Marryat and published in 1847.

10. After Portsmouth FC won the FA Cup in 1939, fixtures were suspended because of the Second World War and the trophy was stowed away in the strongroom in the basement of the Guildhall in Portsmouth until the cessation of hostilities in 1945. For this reason, Portsmouth can claim to have held the FA Cup longer than any football club – technically, the club held the trophy from 1939 until 1945, rather than the usual one year period!

CRONDALL THE FEATHERS 1906 56350

FRANCIS FRITH

PIONEER VICTORIAN PHOTOGRAPHER

Francis Frith, founder of the world-famous photographic archive, was a complex and multi-talented man. A devout Quaker and a highly successful Victorian businessman, he was philosophical by nature and pioneering in outlook. By 1855 he had already established a wholesale grocery business in Liverpool, and sold it for the astonishing sum of £200,000, which is the equivalent today of over £15,000,000. Now in his thirties, and captivated by the new science of photography, Frith set out on a series of pioneering journeys up the Nile and to the Near East.

INTRIGUE AND EXPLORATION

He was the first photographer to venture beyond the sixth cataract of the Nile. Africa was still the mysterious 'Dark Continent', and Stanley and Livingstone's historic meeting was a decade into the future. The conditions for picture taking confound belief. He laboured for hours in his wicker dark-room in the sweltering heat of the desert, while the volatile chemicals fizzed dangerously in their trays. Back in London he exhibited his photographs and was 'rapturously cheered' by members of the Royal Society. His reputation as a photographer was made overnight.

VENTURE OF A LIFE-TIME

By the 1870s the railways had threaded their way across the country, and Bank Holidays and half-day Saturdays had been made obligatory by Act of Parliament. All of a sudden the working man and his family were able to enjoy days out, take holidays, and see a little more of the world.

With typical business acumen, Francis Frith foresaw that these new tourists would enjoy having souvenirs to commemorate their days out. For the next thirty years he travelled the country by train and by pony and trap, producing fine photographs of seaside resorts and beauty spots that were keenly bought by millions of Victorians. These prints were painstakingly pasted into family albums and pored over during the dark nights of winter, rekindling precious memories of summer excursions. Frith's studio was soon supplying retail shops all over the country, and by 1890 F Frith & Co had become the greatest specialist photographic publishing company in the world, with over 2,000 sales outlets, and pioneered the picture postcard.

FRANCIS FRITH'S LEGACY

Francis Frith had died in 1898 at his villa in Cannes, his great project still growing. By 1970 the archive he created contained over a third of a million pictures showing 7,000 British towns and villages.

Frith's legacy to us today is of immense significance and value, for the magnificent archive of evocative photographs he created provides a unique record of change in the cities, towns and villages throughout Britain over a century and more. Frith and his fellow studio photographers revisited locations many times down the years to update their views, compiling for us an enthralling and colourful pageant of British life and character.

We are fortunate that Frith was dedicated to recording the minutiae of everyday life. For it is this sheer wealth of visual data, the painstaking chronicle of changes in dress, transport, street layouts, buildings, housing and landscape that captivates us so much today, offering us a powerful link with the past and with the lives of our ancestors.

Computers have now made it possible for Frith's many thousands of images to be accessed almost instantly. The archive offers every one of us an opportunity to examine the places where we and our families have lived and worked down the years. Its images, depicting our shared past, are now bringing pleasure and enlightenment to millions around the world a century and more after his death.

For further information visit: www.francisfrith.com

INTERIOR DECORATION

Frith's photographs can be seen framed and as giant wall murals in thousands of pubs, restaurants, hotels, banks, retail stores and other public buildings throughout Britain. These provide interesting and attractive décor, generating strong local interest and acting as a powerful reminder of gentler days in our increasingly busy and frenetic world.

FRITH PRODUCTS

All Frith photographs are available as prints and posters in a variety of different sizes and styles. In the UK we also offer a range of other gift and stationery products illustrated with Frith photographs, although many of these are not available for delivery outside the UK – see our web site for more information on the products available for delivery in your country.

THE INTERNET

Over 100,000 photographs of Britain can be viewed and purchased on the Frith web site. The web site also includes memories and reminiscences contributed by our customers, who have personal knowledge of localities and of the people and properties depicted in Frith photographs. If you wish to learn more about a specific town or village you may find these reminiscences fascinating to browse. Why not add your own comments if you think they would be of interest to others? See **www.francisfrith.com**

PLEASE HELP US BRING FRITH'S PHOTOGRAPHS TO LIFE

Our authors do their best to recount the history of the places they write about. They give insights into how particular towns and villages developed, they describe the architecture of streets and buildings, and they discuss the lives of famous people who lived there. But however knowledgeable our authors are, the story they tell is necessarily incomplete.

Frith's photographs are so much more than plain historical documents. They are living proofs of the flow of human life down the generations. They show real people at real moments in history; and each of those people is the son or daughter of someone, the brother or sister, aunt or uncle, grandfather or grandmother of someone else. All of them lived, worked and played in the streets depicted in Frith's photographs.

We would be grateful if you would give us your insights into the places shown in our photographs: the streets and buildings, the shops, businesses and industries. Post your memories of life in those streets on the Frith website: what it was like growing up there, who ran the local shop and what shopping was like years ago; if your workplace is shown tell us about your working day and what the building is used for now. Read other visitors' memories and reconnect with your shared local history and heritage. With your help more and more Frith photographs can be brought to life, and vital memories preserved for posterity, and for the benefit of historians in the future.

Wherever possible, we will try to include some of your comments in future editions of our books. Moreover, if you spot errors in dates, titles or other facts, please let us know, because our archive records are not always completely accurate—they rely on 140 years of human endeavour and hand-compiled records. You can email us using the contact form on the website.

Thank you!

For further information, trade, or author enquiries please contact us at the address below:

The Francis Frith Collection, Unit 6, Oakley Business Park, Wylye Road, Dinton, Wiltshire SP3 5EU.

Tel: +44 (0)1722 716 376 Fax: +44 (0)1722 716 881
e-mail: sales@francisfrith.co.uk **www.francisfrith.com**